Grammarchants
More Jazz Chants

CAROLYN GRAHAM

Marilyn Rosenthal
Developmental Editor

Oxford University Press

Oxford University Press
200 Madison Avenue
New York, NY 10016 USA

Walton Street
Oxford OX2 6DP England

OXFORD is a trademark of Oxford University Press.

Library of Congress Cataloging-in-Publication Data

Graham, Carolyn.
    Grammarchants — more jazz chants: a review of basic
structures of spoken American English/Carolyn Graham; Marilyn
Rosenthal, developmental editor.
        p. cm.
    Includes index.
    ISBN 0-19-434236-0. — ISBN 0-19-434641-2 (cassette).—
ISBN 0-19-434642-0 (set)—ISBN 0-19-434643-9 (class pack)
    1. English language—Textbooks for foreign speakers. 2. English
language—Spoken English—United States. 3. Jazz vocals —Texts.
4. Americanisms. 5. Chants. I. Rosenthal, Marilyn S., 1940-
    II. Title.
    PE1128.G6484 1993
    428.2′4—dc20
    93-6720
    CIP

Editorial Manager: Susan Lanzano
Developmental Editor: Marilyn Rosenthal, Syntactix International
Content Editor: Helen Munch
Associate Editor: Allen Appel
Production Manager: Abram Hall
Designer: Sharon Hudak

Printing (last digit): 10 9 8 7 6 5 4 3 2

Printed in the United States of America.

Jazz Chants® is a registered trademark of Oxford University Press.

Dedicated to
Little m

Acknowledgments

I wish to thank Helen Munch for her many helpful suggestions and her efforts to make this book a reality.

I would like to express my appreciation to Joey Mennona for his brilliant work in arranging and performing the music and rhythm on the accompanying tape.

Special thanks to Russell Goldberg, Michael Warren-Powell, Rick Sabatini, Daniel J. Sherman, and Mona Stiles.

My gratitude, as always, to Marilyn Rosenthal.

Contents

Introduction
What Is a Grammarchant? xi
The Sounds of American English...xii
Presenting the Chants xiii

Unit 1 **Verb *To Be* *Part One*** 1
Yes/No Questions • Subject Pronouns • Definite/Indefinite Articles •
Plural Nouns

Grammarchant: The Verb *To Be*
1. Are You French?
2. Is There Anybody Here from Thailand?
3. Is Sam Married?
4. Are There Two M's in Grammar?
5. Boxes of Books
Unit 1 Exercises 5

Unit 2 **Verb *To Be* *Part Two***...7
Yes/No Questions • Information Questions • Demonstratives

Grammarchant: Questions with the Verb *To Be*
1. Checklist
2. Where's Mary?
3. This, That, These, Those
4. Checking In at the Airport
5. This Is Wednesday, Isn't It?
Unit 2 Exercises 11

Unit 3 **Present Continuous** 13
Information Questions • Object Pronouns

Grammarchant: The Verb *To Be* + *I-N-G*
1. What's Going On This Morning?
2. When Are You Leaving?
3. What's She Doing?
4. Are You Coming with Us?
5. Is She Still Married to Bobby?
Unit 3 Exercises 17

Unit 4 **Simple Present *Part One***..19
Object Pronouns • Yes/No Questions • *Do/Does* • Time Expressions

Grammarchant: Third Person *S*
1. The Love/Hate Song
2. Are You a Student? (song)
3. Couch Potato
4. Do You Always Get Up Early? (song)
5. He Loves the Ocean (song)
Unit 4 Exercises 23

Unit 5   **Simple Present** *Part Two*..................................25
Information Questions • Possessive Pronouns • Possessive Adjectives •
Adverbs of Frequency

Grammarchants: *Do/Does*
1. When Do You Usually Have Breakfast?
2. Relationships (song)
3. Habits
4. He Never Speaks English in His English Class
5. Mistaken Identity
Unit 5 Exercises 29

Unit 6   **Simple Past** *Part One*..................................31
Verb *To Be* • Past Continuous

Grammarchant: Simple Past of the Verb *To Be*
1. I Was There
2. Where Were You in '62?
3. Wasn't That a Beautiful Wedding?
4. Who Was That Man You Were Talking To?
5. It Was Raining When She Saw Him
Unit 6 Exercises 35

Unit 7   **Review**...37
Verb To Be • Contractions • Simple Present • Present Continuous •
Simple Past

Grammarchant: Contractions with *To Be*
1. Her Laundry Is in the Laundry Bag
2. Yesterday It Rained and Rained
3. Wasn't That a Shame?
4. Where's Jack? What's He Doing?
5. Look! The Leaves Are Starting to Fall
Unit 7 Exercises 41

Unit 8   **Simple Past** *Part Two* 43
Information Questions • Regular Verbs • Irregular Verbs • Past Continuous

Grammarchant: Irregular Verbs
1. Saturday Morning
2. What's the Matter with Bob?
3. How Did You Do on the TOEFL Test?
4. Logical Questions
5. I Got a Fax from Max
Unit 8 Exercises 47

Unit 9   **Future** *Be + Going To* 49
Should • *Ought To*

Grammarchant: *Be + Going To* Future
1. What About Me?
2. Are You Going to Go with Joe?
3. Hurry Up, Kate!
4. You Ought to Call Your Mother
5. What Should I Do?
Unit 9 Exercises 53

Unit 10   Future *Will* 55
Let's/Shall • Present Continuous Used as Future

Grammarchant: The Future with *Will*
1. Don't Worry, I'll Do It
2. I Hope Jack'll Be There
3. Let's Try
4. I Hope He Won't Be Homesick
5. Let's Go Out
Unit 10 Exercises 59

Unit 11   *Can/Can't* 61
Have To • *Have Got To*

Grammarchants: No *S* with *Can*
1. Can't Stay, Gotta Go
2. Can't You Stay for a While?
3. This Can't Be Right
4. We've Gotta Get Going
5. When Do We Have to Be Back?
Unit 11 Exercises 65

Unit 12   Comparatives 67
Regular • Irregular

Grammarchant: *E-R, I-E-R*
1. Things Are Getting Better
2. Your Cold Is Getting Worse
3. Used Car Salesman
4. Life Is Getting More and More Complicated
5. The Rich Are Getting Richer
Unit 12 Exercises 71

Unit 13   Present Perfect 73
Regular/Irregular Past Participles • *Ever/Never*

Grammarchant: Irregular Past Participles
1. Have You Ever Been to Boston? (song)
2. I've Never Been to Peru, Have You? (song)
3. California Roll (song)
4. Have You Heard the News?
5. Have You Heard from Mary Lately?
Unit 13 Exercises 77

Unit 14   Unit 14 Superlatives 79
Regular • Irregular

Grammarchant: *E-S-T*
1. I'll Climb the Highest Mountain
2. He Works Like a Dog
3. Mutual Admiration
4. That's the Funniest Thing You've Ever Said
5. He's Not the Best
Unit 14 Exercises 83

Unit 15

Unit 15 Review 85

Simple Present • Simple Past • Present Perfect • *Let's* • Present Continuous • Future *Be + Going to* • *Have to* • Future *Will*

Grammarchant: Short Answer Chant
1. She Loves Him, but He Doesn't Love Her
2. What Do You Want to Do?
3. When It's Midnight in Osaka (song)
4. Oh No, We Missed the Bus!
5. What's the Matter? You Look Tired
Unit 15 Exercises 89

Answer Key 91

Grammarchant Index 94

Structure Index...96

What Is a Grammarchant?

A grammarchant is a rhythmic exercise which presents some aspect of American English grammar and offers students an enjoyable way to reinforce basic principles of the spoken language.

Just as the basic functions of American English were explored in *Small Talk* (Oxford University Press, 1986), *Grammarchants* presents a collection of jazz chants designed to focus on the basic structures appropriate to a class of low-intermediate adult learners, the type of student Carolyn Graham works with at New York University and Harvard.

Each unit opens with a formal grammarchant which presents a basic aspect of grammar, such as the formation of the present continuous tense (verb *to be* + *i-n-g*). The chants in each unit are all written to practice and reinforce the items listed on each unit opener page.

The Sounds of American English

American English stretches, shortens, blends, and often drops sounds. These subtle features of the language are extremely difficult for students to comprehend unless their ear has been properly trained to understand the language of an educated native speaker in natural conversation. The question "Jeet yet?" is meaningless unless one has acquired the listening comprehension skills necessary to connect the sound with the words Did you eat yet? Other examples of the blending of sounds are I'm going to (gonna), I've got to (gotta), and I have to (hafta) go. Students should be aware that the written words gonna, gotta, and hafta would be considered nonstandard English, whereas the spoken forms are perfectly acceptable in American conversation.

A comparison of the text of *Grammarchants* and its cassette helps to illustrate this striking difference between the written word and its spoken form. Jazz chants are particularly useful in developing these listening comprehension skills.

Presenting the Chants

Jazz chants are based on a combination of repetition and learned response. The essential element in presenting a chant is to maintain a clear, steady beat and rhythm.

Initially, the students should repeat the lines of the chant following a model provided by the teacher and/or the cassette. Once the students are familiar with the material, they should progress from a simple choral repetition of a phrase to giving a group response in answer to a question or statement. This step introduces an important new element as the class is now engaged in a dialogue with the teacher. This dialogue may then be transformed into a three- or four-part exchange.

Many of the chants lend themselves to role playing, which enables the students to move from the formal structure of the chants to an informal classroom improvisation, using what they have learned in a situational context. These improvisations give the students not only the opportunity to speak individually but to make choices of attitude in their responses. During the role playing, it is important to make sure that the students retain the rhythm and intonation patterns established earlier.

Verb *To Be* PART ONE

Yes/No Questions • Subject Pronouns • Definite/Indefinite Articles • Plural Nouns

Grammarchant

The Verb *To Be*

Don't forget me!
I'm the verb *to be*.
I'm very important
As you will see.
Don't! Please.
Don't forget me!
Don't forget me,
I'm the verb *to be*.

GRAMMARNOTES

1 Are You French?

This chant offers practice in Yes/No questions, negative short responses, and positive statements. It also provides a review of subject pronouns contracted with the verb *to be.* Note the rising intonation pattern of the Yes/No question. This chant works well as a first week "getting to know you" activity.

2 Is There Anybody Here from Thailand?

This chant provides practice in Yes/No questions using *Is there/Are there* and the use of *any/anybody/anyone*, as well as the noun *student* in singular/plural form. Students should note the rising intonation pattern of the Yes/No question, contrasted with the falling intonation pattern of the statement. This chant is another useful first week activity. If students are from the same country, you might substitute cities for countries.

1 Are You French?

Are you French?
 No, I'm not. I'm Italian.
Is he Korean?
 No, he's not. He's Japanese.
Is she Spanish?
 No, she's not. She's Venezuelan.
Are they Indonesian?
 No, they're not. They're Taiwanese.

2 Is There Anybody Here from Thailand?

Is there anybody here from Thailand?
Are there any students here from Peru?
Is there anybody here from Tahiti?
Is anyone from Katmandu?

Is there anybody here from Bali?
Are there any students here from Rome?
Is there anybody here from Quito?
Are there any students here from Nome?

There's one student here from Thailand.
There are two students here from Peru.
There are three students here from Tahiti.
There's no one here from Katmandu.

3 Is Sam Married?

This chant reviews Yes/No questions followed by negative short responses. It also practices subject pronouns contracted with the verb *to be* and provides vocabulary describing personal relationships.

4 Are There Two M's in Grammar?

This chant offers additional practice in the Yes/No questions using *Is there/Are there.* It also introduces the indefinite articles *a/an* and includes examples of the preposition *in.*

3 Is Sam Married?

Is Sam married?
> No, he's not. He's single.

Is Anne married?
> No, she's not. She's divorced.

Are the Browns divorced?
> No, they're not. They're separated.

Are Bill and Sue in love?
> No, they're not. They're just good friends.

4 Are There Two M's in Grammar?

Are there two m's in grammar?
> Yes, there are.

Is there a k in mistake?
> Yes, there is.

Is there a b in dumb?
> Yes, there is.

Is there a p in stupid?
> Yes, there is.

Are there two l's in silly?
> Yes, there are.

Is there an r in word?
> Yes, there is.

Is there an o in hot?
> Yes, there is.

Is there an n in not?
> Yes, there is.

This chant practices two plural forms— -s (books) and -es (boxes)—and illustrates the use of prepositions with the definite article *(in the/on the/to the)*. It also introduces contrasting adjectives *big/small, old/new.*

5 Boxes of Books

Boxes and boxes and boxes of books.
Big books, small books,
old books, new books.
Books on the bookshelf.
Books on the floor.
Books on the table
next to the door.
Books in the kitchen.
Books in the hall.
Books in the bedroom,
big and small.

Unit 1 Exercises

Exercise 1

Listen carefully as your teacher reads the sentences below. Then listen again as your teacher repeats them. Fill in the blanks with the correct words. Check your answers in the Answer Key, page 91.

1. _____ _____ French _____?

2. No, _____ _____. _____ Italian.

3. _____ _____ Indonesian? No, _____

   _____. _____ Taiwanese.

4. _____ she _____ English _____?

5. _____ there _____ _____ here _____ Peru?

6. _____ _____ two _____ here _____ Italy.

7. _____ _____ _____ k _____ mistake?

8. _____ _____ two l's _____ silly?

9. _____ they _____? No, _____ _____

   _____ separated.

10. _____ _____ _____ women _____

    China _____ _____ _____?

Exercise 2

Listen to your teacher read the sentences below. Listen carefully to the noun ending. If the noun is singular, say "one." If the noun is plural, say "two."

Example: Teacher: The boy<u>s</u> are here.

Student: Two.

Now close your books and listen to your teacher.

1. The book's here.
2. The books are here.
3. The girls are smart.
4. The girl's smart.
5. The tickets are expensive.
6. The ticket's expensive.

Exercise 3

INTERVIEW: Ask your partner the following questions and check (√) the answers in the spaces provided.

	YES	NO
1. Are you Spanish?	☐	☐
2. Are you a student?	☐	☐
3. Is your mother over sixty?	☐	☐
4. Are there any teachers in your family?	☐	☐
5. Are you married?	☐	☐
6. Is there anyone in our class from Japan?	☐	☐
7. Is the teacher from California?	☐	☐
8. Are there any young children in your family?	☐	☐
9. Are your grandparents living?	☐	☐
10. Are any of the students absent today?	☐	☐

Now write your partner's answers on a separate piece of paper. Use complete sentences.

Example: She's not Spanish.

Verb *To Be* *PART TWO*

Yes/No Questions • Information Questions • Demonstratives

Grammarchant

Questions with the Verb *To Be*

Am I? Are you?
Is he? Is she?
We're the Yes/No
questions
of the verb *to be*.
Where are you?
Where is he?
We're the information
questions
of the verb *to be*.

1 Checklist

This chant offers additional practice in Yes/No questions using singular and plural forms. Students should note the plural nouns *students/lights* and the use of the subject pronouns *it/they*.

2 Where's Mary?

This chant provides examples of information questions using *Where.* Students should note that the falling intonation pattern of these questions differs from the rising intonation pattern of Yes/No questions. Students should also note the rising intonation pattern of *Mary who?*

1 Checklist

Are the lights on?
> Yes, they are.

Is the blackboard clean?
> Yes, it is.

Is there chalk on the blackboard?
> Yes, there is.

Are the students here?
> Yes, they are.

Is the teacher here?
> Yes, she is.

Is it time to begin?
> Yes, it is.

2 Where's Mary?

Where's Mary?
> Mary who?

Mary Brown.
> She's out of town.

Where's Bill?
> He's very ill.

Where's Sue?
> She has the flu.

Where's Ted?
> He's home in bed.

Where are Bob and Ray?
> They're absent today.

3 This, That, These, Those

This chant provides practice in the demonstratives *this/that/these/those*. Students should note the plural nouns *fingers/toes/shoulders/knees*. This chant also offers vocabulary to accompany simple movement (*snap/touch/shrug/bend*).

4 Checking In at the Airport

This chant provides examples of Yes/No and information questions, short responses, and positive statements. Students should note the singular/plural contrast (*bag/bags*), the use of the prepositions *in/on/near*, and the identical sounds of *they're/there*.

3 This, That, These, Those

This, that,
these, those.
Snap your fingers,
touch your toes.
This, that,
those, these.
Shrug your shoulders,
bend your knees.

4 Checking In at the Airport

Are the bags all here?
    Yes, they are.
Are the tags on the bags?
    Yes, they are.
Where's the big black bag?
    It's there, on the floor.
Where's the little brown bag?
    It's there, near the door.
Where are the tickets?
    They're there, in your hand.
Where are the tags?
    They're there, on the bags.

This chant offers additional practice in the use of *this/that/these/those*. It also illustrates the use of the tag endings *isn't it/aren't they* with the confirmation *I think it is/ I think so*, and presents the use of the definite article *the*.

5 This is Wednesday, Isn't It?

This is Wednesday, isn't it?
>   I think it is. I think so.

This is the first, isn't it?
>   I think it is. I think so.

Is this the door to the roof?
>   I think so. It must be.

Are these the stairs to the basement?
>   I think so. They must be.

Is that the main entrance to the building?
>   I think so. It must be.

Those are the stairs to the basement, aren't they?
>   I think so. They must be.

That's the exit, isn't it?
>   I think so. It must be.

This is the entrance, isn't it?
>   I think so. It must be.

Unit 2 Exercises

Exercise 1

Listen carefully as your teacher reads the sentences below. Then listen again as your teacher repeats them. Fill in the blanks with the correct words. Check your answers in the Answer Key, page 91.

1. _____ _____ _____ here?

2. _____ _____ chalk _____ _____ blackboard?

3. _____ the _____ _____?

4. Where _____ _____ _____?

5. _____ _____ much _____ long.

6. _____ _____ not _____ size.

7. Where _____ _____ _____?

8. _____ _____, _____ _____ bags.

9. Are _____ _____ _____ _____

   _____ basement?

10. _____ _____ exit, _____ _____?

Exercise 2

Listen to your teacher read five questions from the Answer Key, page 91. Answer each question with a positive short answer using *it, they,* or *there.* Then check your answers on page 91.

1. Yes, _____.

2. Yes, _____.

3. Yes, _____.

4. Yes, _____.

5. Yes, _____.

Exercise 3

INTERVIEW: Ask your partner the following questions and check (√) the answers in the spaces provided.

	YES	NO
1. Are you good in math?	☐	☐
2. Are you shy in the classroom?	☐	☐
3. Is the teacher over twenty-one?	☐	☐
4. Are there more than fifteen students in this class?	☐	☐
5. Is there a clock on the wall in the classroom?	☐	☐
6. Is your desk next to a window?	☐	☐
7. Is it difficult to get a teaching job in your country?	☐	☐
8. Is there a large university in your home town?	☐	☐
9. Are teachers well paid in your country?	☐	☐
10. Are there many women professors in your country?	☐	☐

Now write your partner's answers on a separate piece of paper. Use complete sentences.

Example: He's good in math.

Unit 3
Present Continuous

Grammarchant

The Verb
To Be + *I-N-G*

Remember me?
I'm the verb *to be*.
    Don't forget me!
    I'm the *i-n-g*.
We go together
like A B C.
The verb *to be*
and the *i-n-g*.

1 What's Going On This Morning?

This chant introduces the present continuous in statements and information questions using the question words *What* and *How*. Students should note the singular/plural forms *The water is/The plants are*, which are generally contracted in spoken English. This chant also illustrates the use of the definite article *the*.

1 What's Going On This Morning?

The earth is turning,
The toast is burning,
The water is boiling,
The tea kettle's whistling,
The faucet is leaking,
The floor is creaking,
The plants are dying,
The kids are crying.

What's burning?
    The toast is burning.
What's boiling?
    The water is boiling.
How are the plants?
    The plants are dying.
How are the kids?
    The kids are crying.

2 When Are You Leaving?

This chant introduces the use of the present continuous to talk about future activities. This pattern is very often used with verbs showing movement (*go/come/leave/move/start/finish*). Students should note the question words *When/How/Where*, which are usually contracted with *is/are* in spoken English.

2 When Are You Leaving?

When are you leaving?
    I'm leaving in July.
How are you going?
    I'm planning to fly.
Where is Bob going?
    He's going to Spain.
How is he going?
    He's taking a plane.
Are you leaving next summer?
    I'm leaving next fall.
Are you going with Bobby?
    I'm going with Paul.

3 What's She Doing?

This chant offers additional practice in the information question/statement pattern using the present continuous form. Students should note the dropped *h* in the pronunciation of *What's he*. This chant also provides examples of the vowel reduction in the preposition *to*. Students should also note that the phrase *What are* is usually contracted to *What're* in spoken English.

4 Are You Coming with Us?

This chant illustrates Yes/No and information questions and positive statements using the present continuous form. It also provides examples of the object pronouns *us/me/him/you/them*. Students should note that *How about* and *What about* are interchangeable in this context.

3 What's She Doing?

What's she doing?
    She's writing a book.
What's he doing?
    He's learning to cook.
What are you doing?
    I'm learning to drive.
What are they doing?
    They're learning to dive.
What's Dan doing?
    He's writing a letter.
What's Fran doing?
    She's knitting a sweater.

4 Are You Coming with Us?

Are you coming with us?
    I'm going with Gus.
What about Lee?
    He's coming with me.
What about Tim?
Who's going with him?
    Bob and Jim are going with him.
What about Mary?
Who's going with her?
    I'm not sure who is going with her.
How about Lou?
    He's going with you.
What about Bill?
    He's going with Phil.
How about the Browns?
Who's going with them?
    I think Clem is going with them.

5 Is She Still Married to Bobby?

This chant offers more practice in the present continuous Yes/No question form using *still* to emphasize a continuing activity.

5 Is She Still Married to Bobby?

Is she still married to Bobby?
Is she still living with Fred?
Is she still teaching in London?
Is she still working with Ed?
    Is he still getting his Masters?
    Is he still studying Greek?
    Is he still doing his homework
    every day of the week?
Are you still studying Russian?
Are you still trying to write?
Are you still playing the piano
one hour every night?

Exercise 1

Listen carefully as your teacher reads the sentences below. Then listen again as your teacher repeats them. Fill in the blanks with the correct words. Check your answers in the Answer Key, page 91.

1. _____ he _____?

2. _____ _____ they _____?

3. _____ learning _____ _____.

4. _____ writing _____ letter.

5 _____ toast _____ _____.

6. _____ going _____ this _____?

7. _____ earth _____ _____ and _____

    toast _____ _____.

8. _____ going _____ _____?

9. How _____ _____ _____?

10. _____ _____ still _____ Greek?

Exercise 2

Listen carefully as your teacher reads the sentences from the Answer Key, page 91. When the sentences are repeated, write each one in the space provided. Then answer each question with a short, positive answer. Check your answers on page 91.

1. _____ Yes, _____

2. _____ Yes, _____

3. _____ Yes, _____

4. _____ Yes, _____

5. _____ Yes, _____

Exercise 3

INTERVIEW: Ask your partner the following questions and check (√) or write the answers in the space provided.

	YES	NO
1. Are you taking a course this semester?	☐	☐
2. Are you going to the movies tonight?	☐	☐
3. Are your parents living in a large city?	☐	☐
4. Are things going well for you these days?	☐	☐
5. Are you having any problems with your English?	☐	☐
6. Are you working hard this year?	☐	☐
7. Is your family living in the United States?	☐	☐

8. What are you having for dinner tonight? _____

9. What are you doing after class today? _____

10. Where are you living now? _____

Now write your partner's answers on a separate piece of paper. Use complete sentences.

Example: She's taking a course this semester.

Simple Present *PART ONE*

Object Pronouns • Yes/No Questions • Do/Does • Time Expressions

Grammarchant

Third Person *S*

Third person *s*, yes, yes!
Not in the question, no, no!
Third person *s*, yes, yes!
Not in the negative, no, no!
Third person *s*, yes, yes!
Not in the plural, no, no!
Third person *s*, yes, yes!
Third person *s*. Yes!

1 The Love/Hate Song

This chant provides practice in the third person *s* simple present *(loves/hates)*, and in subject and object pronouns. This chant is also presented as a song on the tape accompanying *Grammarchants*.

2 Are You a Student? (song)

This chant presents Yes/No questions and short responses using *be*, *do*, and *can*. It contrasts *Yes, I am* with *Yes, I can*, and *Yes, I do*. It also offers a useful expression to describe limited language ability: *Yes, I do, but not very well*.

This chant is also presented as a song on the tape accompanying *Grammarchants*. On the tape, the first stanza is repeated.

1 The Love/Hate Song

She loves him.
He loves her.
We love them and they love us.
I love him.
He loves me.
We love everybody.

She hates him.
He hates her.
We hate them and they hate us.
I hate him.
He hates me.
We hate everybody.

2 Are You a Student? (song)

Are you a student?
    Yes, I am.
Can you understand me?
    Yes, I can.
Do you speak English?
    Yes, I do, but not very well.

Is he a student?
    Yes, he is.
Does she speak Spanish?
    Yes, she does.
Do they speak English?
    Yes, they do, but not very well.

3 Couch Potato

This chant offers practice using the simple present tense in questions and positive and negative statements. It also illustrates the use of the infinitive form after *like (Do you like to ski?)*. Note the use of the verb *to be (I'm a/He's a)* contrasted with the verb *to like (I like/He likes)*. This chant should be repeated with other subject pronouns, such as *Does she* or *Do they*.

4 Do You Always Get Up Early? (song)

This chant provides practice with Yes/No questions in the simple present and short responses using *do/does*. It also practices the possessive adjectives *your/her*. Students should note the use of *I do, too* to indicate agreement and the position of the frequency word *always*. This chant is also presented as a song on the tape accompanying *Grammarchants*.

3 Couch Potato

Do you like to swim?
Do you like to ski?
    I'm a couch potato.
    I like TV.
Does he like to swim?
Does he like to ski?
    He's a couch potato.
    He likes TV.
    He doesn't like to swim.
    He doesn't like to ski.
    He's a couch potato.
    He likes TV.

4 Do You Always Get Up Early? (song)

Do you always get up early?
    Yes, I do. Yes, I do.
Do you always get up early?
    Yes, I do.
Does he always get up early?
    Yes, he always gets up early.
    Yes, he gets up very early.
I do, too.
Do you always fix your breakfast?
    Yes, I do. Yes, I do.
Do you always fix your breakfast?
    Yes, I do.
Does she always fix her breakfast?
Does she always fix her breakfast?
    Yes, she always fixes breakfast.
I do, too.

5 He Loves the Ocean (song)

This chant offers practice in simple present third person singular in statements *(he/she loves/likes)*. It also provides a review of the subject pronouns *he/she/they* and illustrates the use of the definite article *the.* Students should note the plural nouns *mountains/clouds/crowds.* This chant is also presented as a song on the tape accompanying *Grammarchants.*

5 He Loves the Ocean (song)

He loves the ocean.
He loves the sky.
She loves to travel.
She loves to fly.
He likes the country.
He loves the clouds.
She likes the city.
She loves the crowds.
She loves the telephone.
She loves to talk.
He loves the mountains.
He loves to walk.
She loves to travel.
She loves to fly.
He loves the ocean.
He loves the sky.

Unit 4 Exercises

Exercise 1

Listen carefully as your teacher reads the sentences below. Then listen again as your teacher repeats them. Fill in the blanks with the correct words. Check your answers in the Answer Key, page 91.

1. _____ _____ like _____ swim.

2. _____ _____ like _____ ski?

3. _____ _____ always _____ _____ early?

4. _____ _____ always _____ _____ breakfast?

5. He _____ _____ mountains.

6. _____ _____ understand me?

7. _____ _____ _____ student?

8. _____ _____ up _____ early.

9. _____ _____ _____ walk.

10. _____ _____ like _____ ocean?

Exercise 2

Listen to your teacher read the questions below. Then complete the short responses in the spaces provided.

1. Are you a student?   Yes, _____ _____.

2. Can he understand me?   Yes, _____ _____.

3. Does he speak English?   Yes, _____ _____.

4. Does she like to ski?   No, _____ _____.

5. Do they like TV?   No, _____ _____.

6. Are they good students?   Yes, _____ _____.

Exercise 3

INTERVIEW: Ask your partner the following questions and check (√) the answers in the spaces provided.

	YES	NO
1. Do you like to study?	☐	☐
2. Do you speak Spanish?	☐	☐
3. Do you always have coffee in the morning?	☐	☐
4. Are you a good cook?	☐	☐
5. Do you like to talk in the morning at breakfast?	☐	☐
6. Do you watch the news every day?	☐	☐
7. Do you like to travel?	☐	☐
8. Does your mother work outside her home?	☐	☐
9. Is your father athletic?	☐	☐
10. Do you read a newspaper in English every day?	☐	☐

Now write your partner's answers on a separate piece of paper. Use complete sentences.

Example: He doesn't like to study.

Unit 5
Simple Present *PART TWO*

Information Questions • Possessive Pronouns • Possessive Adjectives • Adverbs of Frequency

Grammarchant

Do/Does

Four little letters,
does, does.
Looks like goes,
sounds like was.
Two little letters,
do, do.
Looks like go,
sounds like who.

This chant illustrates information questions using *When/What time/What/How long* in the simple present. Students should note the position of the frequency word *usually* and the expression *at most*.

2 Relationships (song)

This chant practices the possessive adjectives *my/his/her/our/their* and presents useful vocabulary describing relationships. This chant is also presented as a song on the tape accompanying *Grammarchants*.

1 When Do You Usually Have Breakfast?

When do you usually have breakfast?
    I usually have breakfast at eight.
What time do you get to the office?
    I'm usually a little bit late.
What do you have for breakfast?
    I usually have coffee and toast.
How long does it take to fix breakfast?
    It takes ten minutes at most.

2 Relationships (song)

He's my teacher.
I'm his student.
She's my neighbor.
I'm her pal.
He's her doctor.
She's his patient.
He's her boyfriend.
She's his gal.

She's my lawyer.
I'm her client.
He's my neighbor.
I'm his friend.
They're our colleagues.
We're together
in our office
to the end.

3 Habits

3 Habits

This chant practices the simple present third person *s* form (*gets/wakes/sleeps/drinks/has/puts/walks*) and the *es* form (*uses*). Students should note the use of the frequency words *always/never/rarely*, the prepositions *on* and *around*, and the possessive adjective *his*.

Bob gets up at six o'clock.
He never wakes up late.
He always gets up early.
He never sleeps till eight.
He always drinks his coffee black.
He never uses cream.
He rarely has a sleepless night.
He never has a dream.
He does his breakfast dishes,
then puts them on the shelf,
walks around the kitchen
humming to himself.

4 He Never Speaks English in His English Class

4 He Never Speaks English in His English Class

This chant practices the negative form of the simple present. Students should note the difference between *never speaks* and *doesn't speak*. Note the use of the prepositions *in/at*, the definite article *the*, and the expression *at all* to strengthen the negative statement.

He never speaks English in his English class.
He never speaks English at night.
He never says "Good morning" in English.
He never says "Oh, that's right!"
He never says "Good evening" in English.
He never says "Have a nice day."
He never says "Hi, how are you?"
He never says "I'm OK."
He doesn't speak English in the classroom.
He doesn't speak English in the hall.
He never speaks English in his English class.
He never speaks English at all.

This chant illustrates the use of Yes/No questions using *Isn't/Aren't*. It also provides practice in the demonstratives *that/those,* and the *s* in the plural nouns *the Browns/friends/ students*. Students should note the possessive adjectives *his/her/my/their.*

5 Mistaken Identity

Isn't that Jack?

    No, that's Jim.

Isn't that Bob?

    No, that's Tim.

Isn't that Sam and his ex-wife Mary?

    No, that's Sally and her husband Harry.

Isn't that Bobby and his brother Mac?

    No, that's Jimmy and his cousin Jack.

Isn't that Alice and her aunt Christine?

    No, that's Susie and my friend Eileen.

Aren't those the Browns with their friends from Maine?

    No, those are students from the coast of Spain.

Unit 5 Exercises

Exercise 1

Listen carefully as your teacher reads the sentences below. Then listen again as your teacher repeats them. Fill in the blanks with the correct words. Check your answers in the Answer Key, page 91.

1. How long _____ _____ take _____ fix _____?

2. _____ _____ _____ little _____ late.

3. _____ always _____ _____ early.

4. He _____ _____ breakfast _____.

5. _____ _____ _____ _____ _____ shelf.

6. _____ never _____ English ____ _____ English class.

7. _____ _____ Sam _____ _____ ex-wife Mary?

8. _____ _____ _____ usually _____ _____

   breakfast?

9. _____ long _____ ____ take ____ _____ ____

   _____ office?

10. What _____ _____ _____ _____ _____

   _____ end ____ _____ day?

Exercise 2

Listen to your teacher read ten questions from the Answer Key, page 91. Write the first word of each question on the lines below. Then check your answers on page 91.

Example: Teacher: Does he live in Boston?

       Student: Does.

1. _____

2 _____

3. _____

4. _____

5. _____

6. _____

7. _____

8. _____

9. _____

10. _____

Exercise 3

INTERVIEW: Ask your partner the following questions and check (√) the answers in the spaces provided.

	YES	NO
1. Do you enjoy eating alone?	☐	☐
2. Do you usually prepare your own lunch?	☐	☐
3. Do people worry about their weight in your country?	☐	☐
4. Does your father cook?	☐	☐
5. Do most men in your country help their wives with the housework?	☐	☐
6. Do most women drive in your country?	☐	☐
7. Do you enjoy eating out?	☐	☐

8. What time do most people have dinner in your country?

_____

9. What do people usually have for breakfast in your country?

_____

10. How often do you eat out? _____

Now write your partner's answers on a separate piece of paper. Use complete sentences.

Example: He enjoys eating alone.

Unit 6
Simple Past *PART ONE*

Verb *To Be* • Past Continuous

Grammarchant

Simple Past of the Verb *To Be*

I was.
You were.
Was he?
Was she?
That's the simple past
tense of the verb *to be*.

We were.
They were.
Were they?
Were we?
That's the simple past
tense of the verb *to be*.

1 I Was There

This chant practices the statement and question forms of the verb *to be* in the simple past tense. Students should note the vowel reduction in the sound of *was (wz)*.

1 I Was There

I was there.
Where were you?
    I was there.
    Where was Sue?
Sue was there.
Where was Bill?
    He was there.
    Where was Jill?
She was there.
Where was Joe?
    Where was Joe?
    I don't know.

2 Where Were You in '62?

This chant illustrates the use of the simple past of the verb *to be* in questions and positive/negative statements. Students should note the use of the preposition *in* and the expressions *Let's see/I'm not sure.*

2 Where Were You in '62?

Where were you in '62?
    I was in France.
    Where were you?
I was in school.
Where was Lou?
    Lou wasn't born in '62.
Where was Lee in '83?
    Let's see.
    Where was he?
I think he was here,
but I'm not sure.
    Where were you?
In Katmandu.

3 Wasn't That a Beautiful Wedding?

This chant provides practice in the simple past tense of the verb *to be,* negative questions *Wasn't/Weren't,* and positive statements *was/were.* Students should note the *s* in the plural noun *flowers* and the pronunciation of *was* when stressed (*It certainly was*) contrasted with the unstressed *was* (*It wz wonderful.*).

3 Wasn't That a Beautiful Wedding?

Wasn't that a beautiful wedding?
> It certainly was. It was wonderful.

Weren't the flowers lovely?
> They certainly were.

Wasn't the music nice?
> It certainly was.

Wasn't the bride lovely?
> She certainly was.

Wasn't her dress gorgeous?
> It certainly was.

Wasn't the groom handsome?
> He certainly was.

Wasn't the weather fine?
> It certainly was.

Wasn't it a beautiful wedding?
> It certainly was. It was wonderful.

4 Who Was That Man You Were Talking To?

This chant practices the past continuous form (*-ing*) and the simple past tense of the verb *to be.* It also offers examples of the demonstratives *that/those* and the possessive adjectives *my/his.* Students should note the plural nouns *people* and *students.*

4 Who Was That Man You Were Talking To?

Who was that man you were talking to?
> That was my brother Lou.

Who was that woman he was sitting with?
> That was his girlfriend Sue.

Who were those people you were waving to?
> Those were my friends from Maine.

Who was that woman you were talking to?
> That was my student from Spain.

This chant uses the past
continuous to describe
background and the simple past
to indicate action. It includes
the simple past forms *was/were,*
the irregular past forms
saw/met/fell/left, and the regular
past forms *parted/turned.*
Students should note the *s* on
the plural nouns *students/clouds.*

5 It Was Raining When She Saw Him

It was raining when she saw him.
It was raining when they met.
It was pouring when they fell in love,
the streets were dark and wet.

It was raining when they parted.
There were dark clouds in the sky.
It was raining when he left her,
when he turned and said "Good-bye."

Exercise 1

Listen carefully as your teacher reads the sentences below. Then listen again as your teacher repeats them. Fill in the blanks with the correct words. Check your answers in the Answer Key, page 92.

1. _____ _____ _____ beautiful wedding?

2. _____ _____ flowers _____?

3. _____ _____ music _____?

4. Who _____ _____ man _____ _____ talking _____?

5. Who _____ _____ people _____ _____ waving _____ ?

6. _____ _____ raining _____ _____ saw _____.

7. _____ _____ dark _____ _____ _____ sky.

8. _____ _____ pouring _____ _____ fell _____ _____.

9. _____ _____ _____ dark _____ wet.

10. _____ _____ raining _____ _____ left _____.

Exercise 2

Listen to your teacher read ten questions from the Answer Key, page 92. Answer each question with short answer using Yes or No as indicated below. Then check your answers page 92.

1. Yes, _____ _____.

2. Yes, _____ _____.

3. No, _____ _____.

4. Yes, _____ _____.

5. No, _____ _____.

6. Yes, _____ _____.

7. No, _____ _____.

8. Yes, _____ _____.

9. No, _____ _____.

10. Yes, _____ _____.

Exercise 3

INTERVIEW: Ask your partner the following questions and write the answers in the space provided.

1. Where were you in 1982? _____

2. What were you doing there? _____

3. What were you wearing yesterday? _____

4. Were you here last year? _____

5. How was the weather when you got up this morning?

   _____

6. Were all the students in class yesterday? _____

7. Were you home last night? _____

8. Were you nervous on the first day of class? _____

9. Was our teacher late today? _____

10. Was it difficult for you to get up this morning?

   _____

Now write your partner's answers on a separate piece of paper. Use complete sentences.

Example: He was in Boston.

Review

**Verb To Be • Contractions • Simple Present •
Present Continuous • Simple Past**

Grammarchant

Contractions with To Be

I am, I'm
Rhymes with time.
You are, You're
Rhymes with sure.
He is, He's
Rhymes with please.
She is, She's
Rhymes with cheese.
We are, We're
Rhymes with dear.
They are, They're
Rhymes with hair.

1 Her Laundry Is in the Laundry Bag

Her laundry is in the laundry bag.
Her gloves are in the drawer.
Her raincoat is in the closet.
Her shoes are on the floor.

His jacket is on the hanger.
His necktie is on the door.
His pants are in the closet.
His shorts are on the floor.

2 Yesterday It Rained and Rained

Yesterday it rained and rained.
Yesterday it poured.
Yesterday the streets were wet.
The children all were bored.
The people stayed indoors all day.
There wasn't much to do.
At last it stopped. We stepped outside.
A rainbow! There! For you!

This chant practices the simple past tense of the verb *to be* with positive and negative questions (*Wasn't that...?*). It also reviews short responses (*Yes, he /she was*). Students should note the exclamations *Wasn't that a shame!* and *What a shame!*

3 Wasn't That a Shame?

Wasn't that a shame?
    What do you mean?
Bill was ill.
Dick was sick.
Kate was late.
Wasn't that a shame?
    Was Bill really ill?
Yes, he was.
    Was Dick really sick?
Yes, he was.
    Was Kate really late?
Yes, she was.
    What a shame!
    What a shame!

This chant practices the present continuous forms of the verbs *do/fix/try/have/write/take/call*. Students should note the information questions with *Where/What* and the possessive adjectives *our/his/her/their*.

4 Where's Jack? What's He Doing?

Where's Jack? What's he doing?
    He's fixing our VCR.
Where's Bob? What's he doing?
    He's trying to park his car.
Where's Anne? What's she doing?
    She's writing a note to Tim.
Where's Kate? What's she doing?
    She's calling her brother Jim.
Where are the kids? What are they doing?
    They're taking their dog for a walk.
Where are your folks? What are they doing?
    They're having a little talk.

5. Look! The Leaves Are Starting to Fall

This chant practices present continuous statements with both singular and plural forms *(is starting/are starting/is coming/are growing)*. Students should note the plural nouns *leaves/nights/flowers/trees* and the use of the preposition with the definite article *(at the)*.

5 Look! The Leaves Are Starting to Fall

Look! The leaves are starting to fall.
Winter is coming, winter is coming.
Now the nights are growing cold.
Winter is coming soon.
Look at the sky! It's starting to snow.
Winter is here, winter is here.
Look at the sky! Look at the snow!
Winter is here, winter is here.

Look! The snow is starting to melt.
Spring is coming, spring is coming.
Look! The flowers are starting to bloom.
Spring is coming soon.
Look at the trees! Look at the flowers!
Spring is here, spring is here.
Look at the sun! Look at the sky!
Summer is coming soon.

Unit 7 Exercises

Exercise 1

Listen carefully as your teacher reads the sentences below. Then listen again as your teacher repeats them. Fill in the blanks with the correct words. Check your answers in the Answer Key, page 92.

1. _____ laundry _____ _____ _____

   laundry _____.

2. _____ pants _____ _____ _____ closet.

3. Yesterday _____ _____ _____ wet.

4. _____ last _____ _____. We _____ outside.

5. _____ that _____ shame?

6. _____ Jack? _____ _____ doing?

7. _____ trying _____ park _____ car.

8. _____ leaves _____ _____ _____ fall.

9. Look! _____ _____ _____ starting _____

   bloom.

10. Look _____ _____ sun! Look _____ _____ sky!

Exercise 2

Listen to your teacher read five questions from the Answer Key, page 92. Answer each question with the short answer starting with Yes or No, as indicated below. Then check your answers on page 92.

1. Yes, _____.

2. No, _____.

3. Yes, _____.

4. Yes, _____.

5. No, _____.

Exercise 3

INTERVIEW: Ask your partner the following questions and check (√) the answers in the spaces provided.

	YES	NO
1. Are you a neat person?	☐	☐
2. Do you always hang up your clothes?	☐	☐
3. Is your closet well-organized?	☐	☐
4. Do you do your laundry?	☐	☐
5. Does anyone clean your room for you?	☐	☐
6. Are your dresser drawers always neat?	☐	☐
7. Do you like rainy days?	☐	☐
8. Do you have four seasons in your country?	☐	☐
9. Does it ever snow in your country?	☐	☐

10. What's your favorite season? _____

Now write your partner's answers on a separate piece of paper. Use complete sentences.

Example: She isn't a neat person.

Simple Past *PART TWO*

Information Questions • Regular Verbs • Irregular Verbs • Past Continuous

Grammarchant

Irregular Verbs

Say, said.
Stop on red.
Eat, ate.
Don't be late!
Break, broke.
Have a Coke.
Take, took.
Learn to cook.
Speak, spoke.
Tell a joke.
Write, wrote.
Get off the boat!

1 Saturday Morning

This chant practices the past tense forms of the regular verbs *call/talk/play/study/finish/decide* and the irregular verbs *go/take/make/sit/fall/take out/ wake up*. Students should note the use of the prepositions *for* and *to*.

2 What's the Matter with Bob?

This chant practices the simple past forms of the irregular verbs *lose/get/come/break* and the regular verbs *bump/happen*. Students should note the information questions beginning with *What's the matter with/What's wrong with/What happened to*.

1 Saturday Morning

First I called my mother.
We talked for an hour.
Then I played tennis,
went home, and took a shower.
I went to the kitchen,
made a cup of tea,
took out my English book,
and studied carefully.
I finished all my homework
without a mistake.
Then I decided
to take a little break.
I sat down for a minute
to watch TV,
fell asleep, and woke up at three.

2 What's the Matter with Bob?

What's the matter with Bob?
　　He lost his job.
What's wrong with Sue?
　　She got the flu.
What's the matter with Jack?
　　His check came back.
What's wrong with Bill?
　　He got a chill.
What's wrong with Peg?
　　She broke her leg.
What happened to Rose?
　　She bumped her nose.

3 How Did You Do on the TOEFL Test?

This chant provides practice in the simple past form of the irregular verb *do (did)*. It illustrates the use of the subject pronouns *he/she/they* and the object pronouns *him/her/them*. Students should note the use of the information questions *How about/What about.*

3 How Did You Do on the TOEFL Test?

How did you do?

How did you do?

How did you do on the TOEFL test?

    Not very well.

    How about you?

Not very well.

What about him?

How did he do?

How did he do?

How did he do on the TOEFL test?

    Not very well.

    What about her?

    How did she do on the TOEFL test?

Not very well.

Not very well.

How about them?

How did they do?

    Not very well.

    Not very well.

4 Logical Questions

This chant practices the simple past form of the irregular verbs *see/meet/say.* Students should note the possessive adjective *your (your teacher)* contrasted with the possessive pronoun *yours (a friend of yours).* This chant illustrates a common pattern of American speech in which the first speaker makes a simple statement that provokes a question, in contrast to the familiar question/answer pattern.

4 Logical Questions

I saw a friend of yours.

    Who did you see?

I saw Jack Brown at the A&P.

    I met a friend of yours.

Who did you meet?

    I met your teacher on Bleeker Street.

    She talked about you.

What did she say?

    She said you spoke very well yesterday.

5 I Got a Fax from Max

This chant practices the simple past with the past continuous to describe future plans *(He said he was going.)*. It also presents the exclamations *What a surprise! What a kick! What a shock!*

5 I Got a Fax from Max

I got a fax from Max!
    What did he say?
He said he was going to the zoo today.
    I got a call from Paul.
What did he say?
    He said he was leaving for L.A. today.
I got a cable from Mabel.
    What did she say?
She said she was coming for a visit in May.
    What a surprise! A fax from Max!
What a kick! A call from Paul!
    What a shock! A cable from Mabel.

Unit 8 Exercises

Exercise 1

Listen carefully as your teacher reads the sentences below. Then listen again as your teacher repeats them. Fill in the blanks with the correct words. Check your answers in the Answer Key, page 92.

1. _____ I _____ _____ mother and we _____ _____ _____ hour.

2. _____ I _____ tennis, _____ home, _____ _____ _____ shower.

3. I _____ _____ _____ homework _____ _____ mistake.

4. _____ I _____ to take _____ _____ break.

5. _____ _____ matter _____ Bob?

6. _____ lost _____ job.

7. How _____ _____ _____ _____ _____ TOEFL test?

8. _____ _____ _____. How _____ _____?

9. I _____ _____ teacher _____ Bleeker Street.

10. She _____ you _____ very well _____.

Exercise 2

Close your book while your teacher reads the following statements. On a separate piece of paper write the logical question in response to each statement. Check your answers in the Answer Key, page 92.

1. I saw a friend of yours last night.

2. Jack said something nice about you yesterday.

3. Oh no! I lost it.

4. He broke something very important to me.

5. She lost a lot of money.

6. I found a strange thing on the street.

7. He gave me a wonderful present.

8. I saw a terrific movie last night.

9. I read a wonderful book last night.

10. I ate something delicious yesterday.

Exercise 3

INTERVIEW: Ask your partner the following questions and write the answers in the space provided.

1. How much money did you spend today? _____

2. Where did you have dinner last night? _____

3. What did you eat for lunch today? _____

4. What did you wear yesterday? _____

5. What was Mary wearing when you saw her? _____

6. How many umbrellas did you lose last year? _____

7. When did you get up this morning? _____

8. What were you thinking about when you woke up this morning?

_____

9. How did you get to school today? _____

10. How long did it take you to come to school today? _____

Now write your partner's answers on a separate piece of paper. Use complete sentences.

Example: He spent four dollars.

Future *Be + Going To*

Should • Ought To

Grammarchant

Be + Going To Future

I am, I'm.
I'm going to go.
I'm gonna, gonna, gonna,
gonna, gonna go.

He is, he's
He's going to go.
He's gonna, gonna, gonna,
gonna, gonna go.

She is, she's.
You are, you're.
We are, we're.
They are, they're.
They're gonna, gonna,
gonna,gonna, gonna go.
They're gonna, gonna,
gonna,gonna, gonna go.

1 What About Me?

This chant practices the future with *be + going to* and illustrates the use of the object pronouns *me/you/us/him/them*. It also illustrates the use of the information question with the expression *What about*.

1 What About Me?

What about me?

What about you?

What about us?

What are we going to do?

> What about Joe?
>
> What about Lou?
>
> What about them?
>
> What are they going to do?

What about Jim?

What about him?

> What about Ted?
>
> What about Fred?

What about Sue?

What about Ann?

What about them?

What are they going to do?

2 Are You Going to Go with Joe?

This chant practices the future with *be + going to*. Students should note the rising intonation pattern of the Yes/No question *Are you going to...?* contrasted with the falling intonation of the information question *Who is going to ride with...?*

2 Are You Going to Go with Joe?

Are you going to go with Joe?

> No.
>
> Joe's going to go with Sue.

Oh, who's going to ride with Bill?

> Will.
>
> Are you going to go with Bess?

Yes.

Who's going to stay with Fay?

> Ray.
>
> Who's going to ride with us?

Gus.

3 Hurry Up, Kate!

This chant practices the future with *be + going to* and the expressions *Hurry up/Come on/Let's go*. Students should note the use of *Let's/Let's not* to offer a suggestion.

4 You Ought to Call Your Mother

This chant illustrates the use of *ought to* as a strong suggestion or obligation with the *be + going to* future used in response. Students should note the use of the possessive adjectives *his/her* and object pronouns *him/her*.

3 Hurry Up, Kate!

Hurry up, Kate, we're going to be late.
Hurry up, hurry up!
Hurry up, Kate!
    Come on, Steve, our plane is going to leave.
    Come on, come on!
    Come on, Steve!
Let's go, Joe. I think it's going to snow.
Let's go, let's go!
Let's go, Joe!
    Let's not fight. We're going to miss our flight.
    Let's not fight!
    Let's not fight!

4 You Ought to Call Your Mother

You ought to call your mother.
    I'm going to.
When are you going to call her?
    Now.
He ought to write his brother.
    He's going to.
When is he going to write him?
    Now.
She ought to call her mother.
    She's going to.
When is she going to call her?
    Now.

5 What Should I Do?

What should I do?

    You ought to ask Sue.

What should we wear?

    You ought to ask Cher.

What should he say?

    He ought to ask Ray.

Who should she tell?

    She ought to ask Nell.

Unit 9 Exercises

Exercise 1

Listen carefully as your teacher reads the sentences below. Then listen again as your teacher repeats them. Fill in the blanks with the correct words. Check your answers in the Answer Key, page 92.

1. _____ _____ _____ go _____ Joe?

2. _____ _____ _____ _____ stay _____ Sue?

3. _____ _____, Steve, _____ plane _____ _____ _____ leave.

4. _____ go, Joe, I think _____ _____ _____ snow.

5. _____ _____ _____ _____ _____ do?

6. _____ _____ _____ call _____ mother.

7. _____ _____ _____ tell _____ husband.

8. _____ _____ _____ write _____ _____ father.

9. _____ _____ _____ tell?

10. What _____ I _____?

Exercise 2

Listen to your teacher read five questions from the Answer Key, page 92. Answer each question with a positive or negative short answer as indicated below. Then check your answers on page 92.

1. Yes, _____.

2. Yes, _____.

3. No, _____.

4. Yes, _____.

5. No, _____.

Exercise 3

INTERVIEW: Ask your partner the following questions and indicate the answers in the space provided.

1. What are you going to do after class today?

2. Are you going to go out tonight?

3. Are you going to take a vacation this year?

4. Where are you going to be tomorrow at 3?

5. I'm not feeling very well. What do you think I should do?

6. I have a terrible cold. What should I do?

7. Mary is feeling very homesick. What do you think she should do?

8. Do you think I ought to look for another apartment or should I stay where I am?

9. Do you think elderly parents should live with their children?

10. Do you think men should learn to cook?

Now write your partner's answers on a separate piece of paper. Use complete sentences.

Example: She's going to the movies.

Unit 10
Future *Will*

Grammarchant

The Future with *Will*

He will, he'll.
She will, she'll.
He'll, she'll.
Future with *will*.
He will, he'll.
She will, she'll.
Future with *will*.
Future with *will*.

1 Don't Worry, I'll Do It

This chant illustrates the use of the future with *will* to make a promise. It provides examples of the contracted forms *I'll/You'll/won't/Don't/That's*. Students should note the negative command *Don't forget* and the expressions *Don't worry/I won't/That's a promise/You can count on me.*

2 I Hope Jack'll Be There

This chant practices the future with *will* and the present continuous used to express future time.

1 Don't Worry, I'll Do It

Don't worry, I'll do it.
That's a promise.
>You will?
Of course I will.
I'll do it. You'll see.
That's a promise.
>Don't forget!
Don't worry, I won't.
That's a promise. You'll see.
You can count on me.

2 I Hope Jack'll Be There

I hope Jack'll be there.
>I'm sure he will.
>But what about you,
>and what about Bill?
We'll be there,
if we possibly can.
What about Ted?
>He's coming with Ann.
>What about Joe?
He's coming with Fran.
What about Bob?
What about Nell?
>Nell's not feeling very well.

3 Let's Try

This chant illustrates the future with *will* used as a promise. Students should note the contractions *I'll/He'll/She'll/ We'll/You'll* and the use of *will* in the full form when it is not followed by another verb *(All right, I will/So will I).*

3 Let's Try

Let's try.
> All right, I will.
> I'll try.
So will I.
I'll try.
> So will he.
> You'll see.
> He'll try.
So will she.
She'll try.
> So will we.
> We'll try.
> You'll see.

4 I Hope He Won't Be Homesick

This chant illustrates the use of the future forms *will/won't.* Students should note the expressions *I hope/I doubt/ I'm sure/I don't think.*

4 I Hope He Won't Be Homesick

I hope he won't be homesick.
I hope he won't feel bad.
I hope he won't be lonely.
I hope he won't feel sad.
> I don't think he'll get homesick.
> I doubt that he'll feel bad.
> I'm sure he won't feel lonely.
> I hope he won't feel sad.

This chant provides practice in the use of *let's* to make a suggestion about the immediate future. Students should also note the possessive *s* in *Mother's* and the *s* in the plural noun *papers*.

5 Let's Go Out

Let's go out.
> Let's stay home.
Let's eat at Mother's.
> Let's eat alone.
Let's call Betty.
> Let's call Fred.
Let's read the papers
and go to bed.
> Let's go running.
> I want to jog.
Let's stay home
and play with the dog.

Exercise 1

Listen carefully as your teacher reads the sentences below. Then listen again as your teacher repeats them. Fill in the blanks with the correct words. Check your answers in the Answer Key, page 92.

1. _____ do _____, _____ see.

2. _____ worry, I _____ forget.

3. _____ hope _____ be _____.

4. _____ sure _____ _____.

5. _____ _____ there _____ _____ _____ can.

6. I _____ _____ _____ _____ homesick.

7. _____ _____ think _____ get _____.

8. _____ eat _____ _____ tonight.

9. _____ _____ promise, _____ see.

10. You _____ count _____ _____.

Exercise 2

Listen to your teacher read five questions from the Answer Key, page 93. Answer each question with a positive or negative short answer, as indicated below. Then check your answers on page 93.

1. Yes, _____.

2. No, _____.

3. Yes, _____.

4. Yes, _____.

5. No, _____.

Exercise 3

INTERVIEW: Ask your partner the following questions and check (√) your answers in the spaces provided.

	YES	NO
1. Will you be here next year?	☐	☐
2. Do you think you'll take another English class next year?	☐	☐
3. Do you think we'll ever learn to speak English?	☐	☐
4. Do you think you will live to be ninety?	☐	☐
5. Do you think you'll be in the United States in twenty years?	☐	☐
6. Do you think you will ever live in your hometown again?	☐	☐
7. Do you think you will have a large family someday?	☐	☐
8. Do you think you will go out tonight?	☐	☐
9. Do you think it'll rain tomorrow?	☐	☐
10. Do you think all of our classmates will be here next year?	☐	☐

Now write your partner's answers on a separate piece of paper. Use complete sentences.

Example: He'll be here next year.

Can/Can't

Have To • Have Got To

Grammarchant

No *S* with *Can*

No *s* with *can*.
   No *s*?
That's right.
He loves to talk.
He can talk all night.
No *s* with *can*.
   No *s*?
That's right.
   He can talk, talk,
   talk, talk, talk all night.

GRAMMARNOTES

1 Can't Stay, Gotta Go

This chant practices *can't* and *have got to.* Students should note that *have got to* is often reduced to *gotta* in spoken American English.

1 Can't Stay, Gotta Go

Can't stay, gotta go.
Can't stay, gotta go.
Gotta go, gotta go, gotta go!
Can't stay.
> O.K.

Gotta go, can't wait.
> You're late.

Gotta go, can't wait.
> Hurry up! You're late.

Gotta run.
> Have fun.

Can't wait.
> You're late.

Gotta go, can't stay.
Gotta go!

2 Can't You Stay for a While?

This chant practices *can't* in questions and *have to* in statements. Students should note the use of *I wish I could* to express polite refusal in response to a question.

2 Can't You Stay for a While?

Can't you stay for a while?
> I wish I could
> but I have to go to work in the morning.

Can't you stay for lunch?
> I wish I could
> but I have to get back to my office.

Can't you take a break?
> I wish I could.

Can't you take a day off?
> I wish I could.

Can't you stay for a while?
> I wish I could
> but I have to go to work in the morning.

3 This Can't Be Right

This chant illustrates the use of *can't/has to/have to/don't have to* in talking about directions.

3 This Can't Be Right

This can't be right.

It has to be wrong.

This trip can't possibly

take this long.

Can't we ask somebody where we are?

Can't we take a rest? Can't we stop the car?

> We don't have to stop.
>
> I know the way.
>
> I take this road almost every day.

4 We've Gotta Get Going

This chant practices *have to/ don't have to/have got to* in statements. It illustrates the contrast between the simple verb *have* and the verb phrase *have to/have got to*. Students should note that *gotta* is an acceptable form of spoken American English, but the correct written form is *have got to*.

4 We've Gotta Get Going

We've gotta get going.

Our plane is going to leave.

We have to be there by seven.

> We have plenty of time.
>
> It's only five.
>
> We don't have to be there till seven.

We've gotta leave now.

> We have plenty of time.

We have to get going.

> We have lots of time.

We have to get moving.

> We have plenty of time.
>
> We don't have to be there till seven.

5 When Do We Have to Be Back?

This chant illustrates the use of *have to* in information questions using *When/How long/How soon*.

5 When Do We Have to Be Back?

When do we have to be back, Jack?

When do we have to be back?

    You have to be back at two, Lou.

    You have to be back at two.

How long do we have to wait, Kate?

How long do we have to wait?

    You have to wait until ten, Ken.

    You have to wait until ten.

How soon do we have to pay, Ray?

How soon do we have to pay?

    Pay as soon as you can, Ann.

    Pay as soon as you can.

Unit 11 Exercises

Exercise 1

Listen carefully as your teacher reads the sentences below. Then listen again as your teacher repeats them. Fill in the blanks with the correct words. Check your answers in the Answer Key, page 93.

1. _____ _____ stay _____ _____ _____?

2. I _____ I _____, _____ I _____ _____ go

   to work _____ _____ morning.

3. _____ we _____ _____ where _____ _____?

4. I _____ _____ road _____ _____ day.

5. _____ trip _____ possibly _____ _____ long.

6. _____ _____ get _____. _____ plane

   _____ _____ _____ leave.

7. We _____ _____ _____ time. We _____

   _____ _____ _____ there _____ seven.

8. _____ _____ _____ have _____ _____

   _____, Jack?

9. You _____ _____ _____ back _____

   _____, Lou.

10. _____ _____ _____ wait _____ ten, Ken.

Exercise 2

Listen to your teacher read five questions from the Answer Key, page 93. Answer each question with a short answer beginning with the words listed below. Then check your answers on page 93.

1. No, _____.

2. Yes, _____.

3. Yes, _____.

4. No, _____.

5. No, _____.

Exercise 3

INTERVIEW: Ask your partner the following questions and check (√) or write the answers in the space provided.

	YES	NO
1. Can you go shopping after class today?	☐	☐
2. Can you go to the library with me tonight?	☐	☐
3. Do you have to go to work tomorrow morning?	☐	☐
4. Can you understand me when I speak quickly?	☐	☐
5. Can most people understand you when you speak English?	☐	☐

6. What time do we have to be here tomorrow? _____

7. What time does our plane leave? _____

8. When do we have to be at the airport? _____

9. How long will it take to get to the airport? _____

10. When do you have to be back at work? _____

Now write your partner's answers on a separate piece of paper. Use complete sentences.

Example: No, she can't.

Comparatives

Regular • Irregular

Grammarchant

E-R, I-E-R

Add *e-r*, cold/colder.
Add *e-r*, old/older.
Add *e-r*, sweet/sweeter.
Add *e-r*, neat/neater.
I-e-r, pretty/prettier.
I-e-r, busy/busier.
I-e-r, funny/funnier.
I-e-r, sunny/sunnier.

This chant provides practice in the comparative forms *better/stronger/easier.* Students should note that while full forms are used in the written language, contracted forms are generally used in spoken American English, as in *Things're getting/homework's getting/writing's getting/ grammar's getting/accent's getting.*

1 Things Are Getting Better

Things are getting better, much better.
Things are getting better every day.
    I'm glad.
The homework is getting easier, much easier.
The homework is getting easier every day.
    That's good.
Your English is improving.
Your writing is getting stronger.
Your grammar is getting better every day.
    Hooray!
Your accent is getting better, much better.
Your accent is getting better every day.
    Hooray!

2 Your Cold Is Getting Worse

This chant practices the irregular comparative forms *good/better* and *bad/worse.* Students should also note the use of *should/ought to.*

2 Your Cold Is Getting Worse

Your cold is getting worse.
You ought to see the nurse.
    Oh no, I'm fine.
    My cold is much better.
Your cough is getting worse.
You ought to see the nurse.
    Oh no, I'm fine.
    My cough is much better.
Your cough sounds bad.
It doesn't sound good.
You ought to see the nurse.
You really should.

3 Used Car Salesman

This chant practices the comparative forms *better/safer/easier* with those of three or more syllables *(more comfortable/more beautiful/more economical)*. Students should note the use of *much more* for emphasis.

4 Life Is Getting More and More Complicated

This chant illustrates the use of the comparative forms *harder/easier/better/simpler/more interesting/more complicated/ more* (and *less*) *difficult*. Students should note the contrast of the singular form with the plural form *Life is/Things are* and the use of the expression *I'll say* to indicate strong agreement.

3 Used Car Salesman

How would you compare them?
>There's really no comparison.
>This one is better than the others.

Which one is safer?
>There's really no comparison.
>This one is safer than the others.
>This one is much more comfortable.
>This one is much more beautiful.
>This one is much more economical.
>This one is easier to drive.

4 Life Is Getting More and More Complicated

Life is getting more and more interesting.
>More difficult,
>more complicated.

Life is getting more and more difficult.

Things are getting harder every day.
>I'll say.

Life is getting more and more interesting.
>Much easier,
>less difficult.

Life is getting more and more interesting.
>Things are getting better every day.

I'll say.

This chant practices the regular comparative forms *richer/poorer/older/colder/taller/smaller/weaker/stronger* and the irregular comparative forms *better/worse*.

5 The Rich Are Getting Richer

The rich are getting richer.
The poor are getting poorer.
  The good are getting better.
  The bad are getting worse.
The old are getting older.
The nights are getting colder.
  The good are getting better.
  The bad are getting worse.
The tall are getting taller.
The small are getting smaller.
  The good are getting better.
  The bad are getting worse.
The weak are getting weaker.
The strong are getting stronger.
  The good are getting better.
  The bad are getting worse.

Unit 12 Exercises

Exercise 1

Listen carefully as your teacher reads the sentences below. Then listen again as your teacher repeats them. Fill in the blanks with the correct words. Check your answers in the Answer Key, page 93.

1. _____ homework _____ _____ every day.

2. _____ English _____ _____ every day.

3. _____ cough _____ bad. You _____ _____ see

   _____ nurse.

4. _____ one _____ _____ _____ comfortable

   _____ _____ _____.

5. Life _____ _____ _____ and _____ interesting.

6. _____ _____ _____ better _____ day.

7. _____ rich _____ _____ _____.

8. The _____ _____ _____ _____.

9. _____ are _____ more _____ _____ _____.

10. _____ bad _____ _____ _____.

Exercise 2

Close your books and listen carefully as your teacher reads the following sentences. Write the answers on a separate piece of paper. Check your answers with the Answer Key, page 93.

1. Mary is 25 years old. Her brother Bob is 19 years old. Compare Mary and her brother in terms of age.

2. Today the temperature is 70°. Yesterday it was 65°. Compare the weather today with the weather yesterday.

3. Last year Bob made $30,000. This year he made $15,000. Compare Bob's salary this year with last year's salary.

4. Ann gets up every day at 7:30 a.m. Bob gets up at 6:00 a.m. Compare Ann and Bob in terms of when they get up.

5. Bill works from 9 to 5 five days a week. Ray works from 8 to 7 six days a week. Compare Bill and Ray in terms of their work schedule.

Exercise 3

INTERVIEW: Ask your partner the following questions and check (√) the answers in the spaces provided.

	YES	NO
1. Is your English improving?	☐	☐
2. Is your accent getting better?	☐	☐
3. Is your writing better today than it was last year?	☐	☐
4. Are rents more expensive here than in your country?	☐	☐
5. Are the streets safer here than in your country?	☐	☐
6. Is your life more interesting today than it was five years ago?	☐	☐
7. Is your life easier today than it was ten years ago?	☐	☐
8. Do you believe that things in general are getting better?	☐	☐
9. Do you agree that the rich are getting richer and the poor are getting poorer?	☐	☐
10. Do you think that education is improving in your country?	☐	☐

Now write your partner's answers on a separate piece of paper. Use complete sentences.

Example: His English is improving.

Present Perfect

Regular/Irregular Past Participles • *Ever/Never*

Grammarchant

Irregular Past Participles

Do, done.
Rhymes with one.
See, seen.
Rhymes with green.
Be, been.
Rhymes with in.
Go, gone.
Rhymes with on.

GRAMMARNOTES

1 Have You Ever Been to Boston? (song)

This chant uses the present perfect question *Have you ever...?* to discuss life experiences, and practices positive and negative short responses *(Yes, I have/No, I haven't)*. This chant is also presented as a song on the tape accompanying *Grammarchants*.

2 I've Never Been to Peru, Have You? (song)

This chant combines the present perfect statement form with a question response as a conversation opener. This chant is also presented as a song on the tape accompanying *Grammarchants*.

1 Have You Ever Been to Boston? (song)

Have you ever been to Boston?
> Yes, I have.
>> No, I haven't.
Have you ever been to Boston?
> Yes, I have.
>> No, I haven't.
Have you ever been to Boston?
Have you ever been to Boston?
Have you ever been to Boston?
> Yes I have.
>> No, I haven't.

Variations: Have you ever worked in Boston?
Have you ever fallen in love in Boston?

2 I've Never Been to Peru, Have You? (song)

I've never been to Peru, have you?
Have you?
If I wake up in Peru, I won't know what to do.
I've never been to Japan, have you?
Have you?
If I wake up in Japan, I won't know where I am.
I've never been to L.A., have you?
Have you?
If I wake up in L.A., I won't know what to say.

3 California Roll (song)

This chant practices present perfect questions and negative statements. Students should note the irregular past participles *eaten/been/had/gone*. Sushi is a popular Japanese food consisting of raw fish and rice. A California roll is a particular kind of sushi served in Japanese restaurants in the U.S. Kimchi is a popular Korean food consisting of spicy pickled cabbage. This chant is also presented as a song on the tape accompanying *Grammarchants*.

3 California Roll (song)

Have you ever eaten sushi?
or a California roll?
Have you ever eaten kimchi?
Have you ever been to Seoul?
    No, I've never eaten kimchi.
    I've never been to Seoul.
    And I've never ever ever had
    a California roll.
Have you ever been arrested?
Have you ever gone to jail?
Have you ever had a diamond ring
or worn a wedding veil?
    No, I've never been arrested.
    I've never gone to jail.
    I've never had a diamond ring
    or worn a wedding veil.
I've never lived in Brooklyn.
I've never lived in Queens.
I've never eaten sushi in a house in New Orleans.
    I've never eaten kimchi.
    I've never been to Seoul.
    And I've never ever ever had a California roll!
    No, I've never ever ever had a California roll!

4 Have You Heard the News?

This chant practices the present perfect with Yes/No questions and information questions.

4 Have You Heard the News?

Have you heard the news about Joe?
> No!

Haven't you heard about Sue?
> Who?

Joe's wife Sue! Haven't you heard?

Sue ran off with Lou.
> Sue and Lou? Oh no!
> What's going to happen to Joe?

I don't know.

Have you heard the news about Lynn?
> No. What about Lynn?

Where have you been?

Everyone knows about Lynn.
> Not me.
> Nobody tells me anything.

5 Have You Heard from Mary Lately?

This chant reviews present perfect questions with the short positive and negative responses *Yes, I have/No, I haven't.* Students should note the change of tenses within one short conversation, starting with a present perfect question to open the conversation, followed by the simple past (to give specific information), and ending with the present continuous (to inquire about the immediate present).

5 Have You Heard from Mary Lately?

Have you heard from Mary lately?
> No, I haven't, have you?

Yes, I have. She called last night.
> How's she doing?

She's doing all right.

Have you spoken to Bobby lately?
> Yes, I have. He called last night.

How's he doing?
> He's doing all right.

Have you talked to Ray?
> Yes, I have.

How's he doing?
> He's doing O.K.

Exercise 1

Listen carefully as your teacher reads the sentences below. Then listen again as your teacher repeats them. Fill in the blanks with the correct words. Check your answers in the Answer Key, page 93.

1. _____ you _____ _____ Boston?

2. _____ never _____ _____ _____ _____

   Boston.

3. _____ never _____ sushi.

4. _____ never _____ _____ Seoul.

5. _____ never _____ _____ diamond ring.

6. _____ you _____ _____ news _____ Joe?

7. _____ _____ you _____?

8. I _____ _____ you _____ _____.

9. _____ you _____ _____ Mary _____?

10. _____ you _____ _____ Bobby _____?

Exercise 2

Listen to your teacher read five questions from the Answer Key, page 93. When your teacher reads the questions a second time, write the complete question in the space provided. Then answer the questions. Check your questions and answers on page 93.

1. _____ Yes, _____.

2. _____ No, _____.

3. _____ Yes, _____.

4. _____ No, _____.

5. _____ No, _____.

Exercise 3

INTERVIEW: Ask your partner the following questions and check (√) the answers in the spaces provided.

	YES	NO
1. Have you ever been to Hollywood?	☐	☐
2. Has anyone ever told you a lie?	☐	☐
3. Have you ever fallen in love with a stranger?	☐	☐
4. Have you ever fallen asleep in a movie?	☐	☐
5. Has anyone ever given you a ring?	☐	☐
6. Have you ever eaten raw fish?	☐	☐
7. Have you ever cooked dinner for twelve people?	☐	☐
8. Have you ever gone to a surprise party?	☐	☐
9. Have you ever broken your arm or leg?	☐	☐
10. Have you ever hurt anybody?	☐	☐

Now write your partner's answers on a separate piece of paper. Use complete sentences.

Example: She's never been to Hollywood.

Unit 14
Superlatives

Grammarchant

E-S-T

E-s-t, e-s-t.
He's the fastest skier in
history.
E-s-t, e-s-t.
She's the strongest
swimmer in the family.
E-s-t, e-s-t.
He's the cutest baby in
the nursery.
E-s-t, e-s-t.
He's the silliest student
in the library.

1 I'll Climb the Highest Mountain

I'll climb the highest mountain.
I'll swim the deepest sea.
I'll walk along the longest road
if you will come with me.

I'll paint the finest painting
for all the world to see.
I'll tell the sweetest story
if you will walk with me.

2 He Works Like a Dog

He works like a dog.
He eats like a horse.
He's the very best student in the English course.
    Does he really work hard?
He works like a dog.
    Does he eat a lot?
He eats like a horse.
        He works like a dog.
        He eats like a horse.
        He's the very best student in the English course.

3 Mutual Admiration

This chant provides examples of the regular superlative forms using *e-s-t (greatest/smartest/ nicest/brightest)* and *most* (with *remarkable/wonderful)*. It also practices the irregular superlative form *best.*

3 Mutual Admiration

She thinks he's the best.
She thinks he's the greatest.
She thinks he's the smartest man in the world.
    He thinks she's the nicest.
    He thinks she's the brightest.
    He thinks she's the kindest woman in the world.
She thinks he's the most remarkable man
in the whole wide world,
in the whole wide world.
    He thinks she's the most wonderful woman
    in the whole wide world,
    in the whole wide world.

4 That's the Funniest Thing You've Ever Said

This chant practices the present perfect combined with the superlative forms *-est/-iest (funny/silly/hard/nice/cheap/ tough/big).*

4 That's the Funniest Thing You've Ever Said

That's the funniest thing you've ever said.
That's the silliest book I've ever read.
That's the hardest thing he's ever done.
That's the biggest prize she's ever won.
That's the cheapest car I've ever bought.
That's the toughest class I've ever taught.
Those are the nicest words you've ever spoken.
That's the biggest promise he's ever broken.

5 He's Not the Best

He's not the best.
He's not the worst.
He's not the last.
He's not the first.
He's in the middle.
He's in between.
He's not too old.
He's just sixteen.

Unit 14 Exercises

Exercise 1

Listen carefully as your teacher reads the sentences below. Then listen again as your teacher repeats them. Fill in the blanks with the correct words. Check your answers in the Answer Key, page 93.

1. _____ climb _____ _____ mountain.

2. _____ swim _____ _____ sea.

3. _____ walk _____ _____ _____ road, _____

    you _____ _____ with me.

4. _____ _____ very _____ student _____ _____ class.

5. She _____ _____ _____ _____ man _____ knows.

6. _____ _____ _____ _____ _____ woman

    _____ _____ world.

7. _____ _____ _____ thing _____ _____ said.

8. _____ _____ _____ thing _____ _____

    _____.

9. _____ _____ _____ _____ words _____

    _____ _____.

10. _____ _____ _____ promise _____ ever _____.

Exercise 2

Listen to your teacher read five questions from the Answer Key, page 93. When your teacher reads the questions a second time, write the complete question in the space provided. Then answer the questions. Check your questions and answers on page 93.

1. _____ No, _____.

2. _____ Yes, _____.

3. _____ Yes, _____.

4. _____ No, _____.

5. _____ Yes, _____.

Exercise 3

INTERVIEW: Ask your partner the following questions. Write the answers in the space provided.

1. Who is the best student in your English class?

2. What's the name of the best university in your country?

3. In your opinion, what is the most difficult profession in the world?

4. Where is the best place to spend a summer holiday?

5. What is the most difficult thing you have ever done?

6. When is the best time to visit your country?

7. What was the easiest subject for you in high school?

8. Who is the most interesting person you have ever met?

9. What is the best age to get married?

10. What is the best thing that ever happened to you?

Now write your partner's answers on a separate piece of paper. Use complete sentences.

Example: Kim is the best student in the class.

Review

**Simple Present • Simple Past • Present Perfect • *Let's* •
Present Continuous • Future *Be + Going to* • *Have to* • Future *Will***

Grammarchant

Short Answer Chant

Yes, I do.
Yes, I am.
Yes, we are.
Yes, we can.
Yes, she has.
Yes, she does.
Yes, he did.
Yes, he was.

GRAMMARNOTES

1 She Loves Him, but He Doesn't Love Her

This chant practices the simple present and simple past in positive and negative statements. It also reviews the expressions *That's too bad! What a shame!* expressing sympathy. Students should note the use of *but* to connect one positive and one negative idea.

2 What Do You Want to Do?

This chant practices information questions using the simple present, followed by *Let's* to make a suggestion, and present perfect statements *I haven't been/seen/taken/done.* Students should note the use of the expression *for ages* to indicate a very long time.

1 She Loves Him, but He Doesn't Love Her

She loves him, but he doesn't love her.
>That's too bad!
>What a shame!

She gave him a book, but he didn't read it.
>That's too bad!
>What a shame!

She bought him a tie, but he didn't wear it.
>That's too bad!
>What a shame!

She loves him, but he loves Kim.
>That's too bad!
>What a shame!

2 What Do You Want to Do?

What do you want to do?
>Let's go to the zoo.
>I haven't been there for ages.

Where do you want to go?
>Let's go to a show.
>I haven't seen a show for ages.

How do you want to go?
>Let's take the bus.
>I haven't taken the bus for ages.

Where do you want to eat?
>Let's eat in the park.
>I haven't done that for ages.

3 When It's Midnight in Osaka (song)

This chant practices the simple present and present continuous. Students should note the use of the preposition *in* with cities or countries *(in Paris/in Korea)*. This chant is also presented as a song on the tape accompanying *Grammarchants*.

4 Oh No, We Missed the Bus!

This chant practices the change of tenses in one conversation from simple past to future with *be + going to* followed by the future with *will* and the simple present. Students should note the use of *have to* to indicate necessity and *hope* to indicate a positive feeling about the future.

3 When It's Midnight in Osaka (song)

When it's midnight in Osaka,
it's morning in L.A.
When the sun comes up in Paris,
they're asleep in Monterrey.

When the sun shines in Korea,
they're sleeping in Peru.
When it snows in New York City,
it's spring in Timbuktu.

4 Oh No, We Missed the Bus!

Oh no! We missed the bus!
How are we going to get back, Jack?
 We'll have to wait for another bus.
 Don't worry, it won't be long.
I hate to wait.
 I know you do,
 but we have to wait, Kate.
I don't want to wait.
 I know you don't,
 but we have to wait, Kate.
How long will it be?
 It won't be long.
I hope you're right.
 I'm never wrong.

**5 What's the Matter?
You Look Tired**

This chant practices the simple present with the simple past. It presents appropriate language to respond to bad news *(Oh no! That's too bad/I'm so sorry to hear that).*

5 What's the Matter? You Look Tired

What's the matter?

You look tired.

You look awful.

    I got fired.

Oh no, that's too bad!

I'm so sorry to hear that!

    What's the matter with Joe?

    He looks tired.

    He looks nervous.

He got fired.

    Oh no! That's too bad.

    I'm so sorry to hear that.

Unit 15 Exercises

Exercise 1

Listen carefully as your teacher reads the sentences below. Then listen again as your teacher repeats them. Fill in the blanks with the correct words. Check your answers in the Answer Key, page 93.

1. She _____ him, but _____ _____ love _____.

2. She _____ _____ _____ tie, but he _____ wear _____.

3. How _____ we _____ _____ get back, Jack?

4. _____ _____ _____ wait _____ another bus.

5. What _____ you _____ _____ do?

6. _____ go _____ _____ zoo.

7. I _____ _____ there _____ ages.

8. Where _____ _____ _____ _____ eat?

9. _____ eat _____ _____ park.

10. I _____ _____ there _____ ages.

Exercise 2

Listen to your teacher read five questions from the Answer Key, page 93. Answer each question with a positive short answer. Then check your answers on page 93.

1. Yes, _____.

2. No, _____.

3. No, _____.

4. Yes, _____.

5. Yes, _____.

Exercise 3

INTERVIEW: Ask your partner the following questions and check (√) or write the answers in the space provided.

	YES	NO
1. Have you ever missed a plane?	☐	☐
2. Do you usually arrive at the airport early?	☐	☐
3. Do you hate to wait?	☐	☐
4. Have you ever been fired?	☐	☐
5. Have you ever quit a job?	☐	☐
6. Do you like to go to the movies?	☐	☐
7. Did you go out last night?	☐	☐

8. How often do you go out to dinner? _____

9. What time is it right now in your hometown?

_____

10. What are people doing right now in your hometown?

_____

Now write your partner's answers on a separate piece of paper. Use complete sentences.

Example: He's never missed a plane.

Answer Key

Unit 1

Exercise 1
1. Are they French students?
2. No, they're not. They're Italian.
3. Is he Indonesian? No, he's not. He's Taiwanese.
4. Is she an English teacher?
5. Are there any students here from Peru?
6. There are two students here from Italy.
7. Is there a k in mistake?
8. Are there two l's in silly?
9. Are they married? No, they're not. They're separated.
10. Are there any women from China in our class?

Unit 2

Exercise 1
1. Is the student here?
2. Is there chalk on the blackboard?
3. Are the lights on?
4. Where are the students?
5. These are much too long.
6. Those are not my size.
7. Where are the tags?
8. They're there, on the bags.
9. Are these the stairs to the basement?
10. That's the exit, isn't it?

Exercise 2
1. Is the light on?   Yes, it is.
2. Are the students here?   Yes, they are.
3. Are the lights on?   Yes, they are.
4. Is there chalk on the blackboard?   Yes, there is.
5. Are there any books on the desk?   Yes, there are.

Unit 3

Exercise 1
1. What's he doing?
2. What are they doing?
3. They're learning to dive.
4. He's writing a letter.
5. The toast is burning.
6. What's going on this morning?
7. The earth is turning and the toast is burning.
8. Who's going with him?
9. How is he going?
10. Is he still studying Greek?

Exercise 2
1. Are the plants dying   Yes, they are.
2. Is the toast burning?   Yes, it is.
3. Are you leaving in July?   Yes, I am.
4. Is he going by plane?   Yes, he is.
5. Is she still studying English? Yes, she is.

Unit 4

Exercise 1
1. He doesn't like to swim.
2. Do you like to ski?
3. Do you always get up early?
4. Does she always fix her breakfast?
5. He loves the mountains.
6. Can you understand me?
7. Are you a student?
8. He gets up very early.
9. She loves to walk.
10. Does he like the ocean?

Exercise 2
1. Yes, I am.
2. Yes, he can.
3. Yes, he does.
4. No, she doesn't.
5. No, they don't.
6. Yes, they are.

Unit 5

Exercise 1
1. How long does it take to fix breakfast?
2. I'm always a little bit late.
3. He always wakes up early.
4. He does his breakfast dishes.
5. He puts them on the shelf.
6. She never speaks English in her English class.
7. Isn't that Sam and his ex-wife Mary?
8. What do you usually have for breakfast?
9. How long does it take to get to the office?
10. What do you usually do at the end of the day?

Exercise 2
1. Is he here?
2. Do you like to ski?
3. Does he speak English?
4. What do you usually have for breakfast?
5. Where do you study English?
6. How long does it take to learn English?
7. Isn't that Jack?
8. Does his wife speak English?
9. Are they still married?
10. Do they live in Boston?

Unit 6

Exercise 1

1. Wasn't that a beautiful wedding?
2. Weren't the flowers lovely?
3. Wasn't the music nice?
4. Who was that man you were talking to?
5. Who were those people you were waving to?
6. It was raining when she saw him.
7. There were dark clouds in the sky.
8. It was pouring when they fell in love.
9. The streets were dark and wet.
10. It was raining when he left her.

Exercise 2

1. Was he busy? — Yes, he was.
2. Were they nervous? — Yes, they were.
3. Was she angry? — No, she wasn't.
4. Was it difficult? — Yes, it was.
5. Were you tired? — No, I wasn't.
6. Was the test difficult? — Yes, it was.
7. Were the students late? — No, they weren't.
8. Was the teacher pleased? — Yes, she was.
9. Were you nervous? — No, I wasn't.
10. Were the questions interesting? — Yes, they were.

Unit 7

Exercise 1

1. Her laundry is in the laundry bag.
2. His pants are in the closet.
3. Yesterday the streets were wet.
4. At last it stopped. We stepped outside.
5. Wasn't that a shame?
6. Where's Jack? What's he doing?
7. He's trying to park his car.
8. The leaves are starting to fall.
9. Look! The flowers are starting to bloom.
10. Look at the sun! Look at the sky!

Exercise 2

1. Was Bill sick yesterday? — Yes, he was.
2. Were the children home last night? — No, they weren't.
3. Is Mary parking her car? — Yes, she is.
4. Are they taking their dog for a walk? — Yes, they are.
5. Is the snow starting to melt? — No, it isn't.

Unit 8

Exercise 1

1. First I called my mother and we talked for an hour.
2. Then I played tennis, went home, and took a shower.
3. I finished all my homework without a mistake.
4. Then I decided to take a little break.
5. What's the matter with Bob?
6. He lost his job.
7. How did you do on the TOEFL test?
8. Not very well. How about you?
9. I met your teacher on Bleeker Street.
10. She said you spoke very well yesterday.

Exercise 2

1. I saw a friend of yours last night.
   Who did you see?
2. Jack said something nice about you yesterday.
   What did he say?
3. Oh no! I lost it.
   What did you lose?
4. He broke something very important to me.
   What did he break?
5. She lost a lot of money.
   How much did she lose?
6. I found a strange thing on the street.
   What did you find?
7. He gave me a wonderful present.
   What did he give you?
8. I saw a terrific movie last night.
   What did you see?
9. I read a wonderful book last night.
   What did you read?
10. I ate something delicious yesterday.
    What did you eat?

Unit 9

Exercise 1

1. Who's going to go with Joe?
2. Are you going to stay with Sue?
3. Come on, Steve, our plane is going to leave.
4. Let's go, Joe, I think it's going to snow.
5. What are they going to do?
6. He ought to call his mother.
7. She ought to tell her husband.
8. He ought to write to his father.
9. Who should she tell?
10. What should I wear?

Exercise 2

1. Are they going to come with us? — Yes, they are.
2. Is Ray going to stay? — Yes, he is.
3. Are we going to ride with Bill? — No, we aren't.
4. Are you going to be there at 6? — Yes, I am.
5. Should I wear a coat? — No, you shouldn't.

Unit 10

Exercise 1

1. I'll do it, you'll see.
2. Don't worry, I won't forget.
3. I hope Jack'll be there.
4. I'm sure he will.
5. We'll be there if we possibly can.
6. I hope they won't be homesick.
7. I don't think he'll get tired.
8. We'll eat at home tonight.
9. That's a promise, you'll see.
10. You can count on me.

Exercise 2

1. Will you call me at 7?	Yes, I will.
2. Will your sister be at the meeting tomorrow?	No, she won't.
3. Will you be at home tonight?	Yes, I will.
4. Will Mr. Brown answer my letter?	Yes, he will.
5. Will your father give me a job?	No, he won't.

Unit 11

Exercise 1

1. Can't you stay for a while?
2. I wish I could, but I have to go to work in the morning.
3. Can't we ask somebody where we are?
4. I take this road almost every day.
5. This trip can't possibly take this long.
6. We must get going. Our plane is going to leave.
7. We have plenty of time. We don't have to be there until seven.
8. When do we have to get back, Jack?
9. You have to be back at two, Lou.
10. You have to wait until ten, Ken.

Exercise 2

1. Can you wait for a while?	No, I can't.
2. Does he have to go to work?	Yes, he does.
3. Can you stay for lunch?	Yes, I can.
4. Do we have to leave now?	No, we don't.
5. Can't she wait for a few minutes?	No, she can't.

Unit 12

Exercise 1

1. The homework is getting easier every day.
2. Your English is improving every day.
3. Your cough sounds bad. You ought to see the nurse.
4. This one is much more comfortable than the others.
5. Life is getting more and more interesting.
6. Things are getting better every day.
7. The rich are getting richer.
8. The poor are getting poorer.
9. Things are getting more and more complicated.
10. The bad are getting worse.

Exercise 2

(There may be more than one correct answer.)
1. Mary is six years older than Bob.
2. It is warmer today than yesterday.
3. Last year Bob made much more money than he did this year.
4. Bob gets up much earlier than Ann every day.
5. Ray works much harder than Bill does.

Unit 13

Exercise 1

1. Have you ever been to Boston?
2. He's never fallen in love in Boston.
3. She's never eaten sushi.
4. They've never been to Seoul.

5. He's never worn a diamond ring.
6. Have you heard the news about Joe?
7. Where have you been?
8. I haven't seen you for ages.
9. Have you heard from Mary lately?
10. Have you spoken to Bobby recently?

Exercise 2

1. Has she ever eaten Korean food?	Yes, she has.
2. Have they ever lived in Boston?	No, they haven't.
3. Has it ever rained in Florida?	Yes, it has.
4. Has he ever been to Disneyland?	No, he hasn't.
5. Has she ever taken an English course?	No, she hasn't.

Unit 14

Exercise 1

1. I'll climb the highest mountain.
2. He'll swim the deepest sea.
3. I'll walk along the longest road, if you will walk with me.
4. He's the very best student in our class.
5. She thinks he's the nicest man she knows.
6. He thinks she's the smartest woman in the world.
7. That's the funniest thing he's ever said.
8. That's the worst thing I've ever heard.
9. Those are the sweetest words I've ever heard.
10. That's the biggest promise he's ever broken.

Exercise 2

1. Has she ever lived in China?	No, she hasn't.
2. Have they ever studied French?	Yes, they have.
3. Has Jack ever eaten yogurt?	Yes, he has.
4. Have the students ever been late to class?	No, they haven't.
5. Has Sue ever given a party?	Yes, she has.

Unit 15

Exercise 1

1. She loves him, but he doesn't love her.
2. She bought him a tie, but he didn't wear it.
3. How are we going to get back, Jack?
4. We'll have to wait for another bus.
5. What do you want to do?
6. Let's go to the zoo.
7. I haven't been there for ages.
8. Where do you want to eat?
9. Let's eat in the park.
10. I haven't eaten there for ages.

Exercise 2

1. Did she buy him a tie?	Yes, she did.
2. Did he wear it?	No, he didn't.
3. Does he love her?	No, he doesn't.
4. Does she love him?	Yes, she does.
5. Are they having problems?	Yes, they are.

Grammarchant Index

Unit 1 Grammarchant
The Verb *To Be*, p. 1

Don't forget me!
I'm the verb *to be*.
I'm very important
As you will see.
Don't! Please.
Don't forget me!
Don't forget me,
I'm the verb *to be*.

Unit 2 Grammarchant
Questions with thé Verb *To Be*, p. 7

Am I? Are you?
Is he? Is she?
We're the Yes/No
questions of the verb *to be*.
Where are you?
Where is he?
We're the information
questions of the verb *to be*.

Unit 3 Grammarchant
The Verb *To Be* + *I-N-G*, p. 13

Remember me?
I'm the Verb *to be*.
    Don't forget me!
    I'm the i-n-g.
We go together
like A B C.
The verb *to be*
and the i-n-g.

Unit 4 Grammarchant
Third Person *S*, p. 19

Third person *s*, yes, yes!
Not in the question, no, no!
Third person *s*, yes, yes!
Not in the negative, no, no!
Third person *s*, yes, yes!
Not in the plural, no, no!
Third person *s*, yes, yes!
Third person *s*. Yes!

Unit 5 Grammarchant
Do/Does, p. 25

Four little letters,
does, does.
Looks like goes,
sounds like was.
Two little letters,
do, do.
Looks like go,
sounds like who.

Unit 6 Grammarchant
Simple Past of the Verb *To Be*, p. 31

I was.
You were.
Was he?
Was she?
That's the simple past
tense of the verb *to be*.
We were.
They were.
Were they?
Were we?
That's the simple past
tense of the verb *to be*.

Unit 7 Grammarchant
Contractions with *To Be*, p. 37

I am, I'm
Rhymes with time.
You are, You're
Rhymes with sure.
He is, He's
Rhymes with please.
She is, She's
Rhymes with cheese.
We are, We're
Rhymes with dear.
They are, They're
Rhymes with hair.

Unit 8 Grammarchant

Irregular Verbs, p. 43

Say, said.
Stop on red.
Eat, ate.
Don't be late!
Break, broke.
Have a Coke.
Take, took.
Learn to cook.
Speak, spoke.
Tell a joke.
Write, wrote.
Get off the boat!

Unit 9 Grammarchant

Be + *Going to* Future. p. 49

I am, I'm.
I'm going to go.
I'm gonna, gonna, gonna,
gonna, gonna go.

He is, he's.
He's going to go.
He's gonna, gonna, gonna,
gonna, gonna go.

She is, she's.
You are, you're.
We are, we're.
They are, they're.
They're gonna, gonna,
gonna, gonna, gonna go.
They're gonna, gonna,
gonna, gonna, gonna go.

Unit 10 Grammarchant

The Future with *Will,* p. 55

He will, he'll.
She will, she'll.
He'll, she'll.
Future with *will.*
He will, he'll.
She will, she'll.
Future with *will.*
Future with *will.*

Unit 11 Grammarchant

No *S* with *Can,* p. 61

No *s* with *can.*
No *s?*
That's right.
He loves to talk.
He can talk all night.
No *s* with *can.*
No *s?*
That's right.
He can talk, talk,
talk, talk, talk all night.

Unit 12 Grammarchant

E-R, I-E-R, p. 67

Add *e-r,* cold/colder.
Add *e-r,* old/older.
Add *e-r,* sweet/sweeter.
Add *e-r,* neat/neater.
I-e-r, pretty/prettier.
I-e-r, busy/busier.
I-e-r, funny/funnier.
I-e-r, sunny/sunnier.

Unit 13 Grammarchant

Irregular Past Participles, p. 73

Do, done.
Rhymes with one.
See, seen.
Rhymes with green.
Be, been.
Rhymes with in.
Go, gone.
Rhymes with on.

Unit 14 Grammarchant

E-S-T, p. 79

E-s-t, est.
He's the fastest skier in history.
E-s-t, e-s-t.
She's the strongest swimmer in the family.
E-s-t, e-s-t.
He's the cutest baby in the nursery.
E-s-t, e-s-t.
He's the silliest student in the library.

Unit 15 Grammarchant

Short Answer Chant, p. 85

Yes, I do.
Yes, I am.
Yes, we are.
Yes, we can.
Yes, she has.
Yes, she does.
Yes, he did.
Yes, he was.

Structure Index

Adverbs of frequency
Do You Always Get Up Early? 21
When Do You Usually Have Breakfast? 26
Habits 27
He Never Speaks English in His English Class 27
This Can't Be Right 63
Have You Ever Been to Boston? 74
I've Never Been to Peru, Have You? 74
California Roll 75

Articles: a/an
Are There Two M's in Grammar? 3
When Are You Leaving? 14
What's She Doing? 15
Couch Potato 21
Wasn't That a Beautiful Wedding? 33
Wasn't That a Shame? 39
Saturday Morning 44
Logical Questions 45
I Got a Fax From Max 46
He Works Like a Dog 80

Articles: the
Is Sam Married? 3
Boxes of Books 4
Checklist 8
Where's Mary? 8
Checking In at the Airport 9
This is Wednesday, Isn't It? 10
What's Going On This Morning? 14
Is She Still Married to Bob? 16
He Loves the Ocean 22
Wasn't That a Beautiful Wedding? 33
Her Laundry Is in the Laundry Bag 38
Yesterday It Rained and Rained 38
Look! The Leaves Are Starting to Fall 40
How Did You Do on the TOEFL Test? 45
The Rich Are Getting Richer 70
That's the Funniest Thing You've Ever Said 81

Comparatives/Superlatives
Things Are Getting Better 68
Your Cold is Getting Worse 68
Used Car Salesman 69
Life is Getting More and More Complicated 69
The Rich Are Getting Richer 70
I'll Climb the Highest Mountain 80
He Works Like a Dog 80
Mutual Admiration 81
That's the Funniest Things You've Ever Said 81
He's Not the Best 82

Conditional
I've Never Been to Peru, Have You? 74
I'll Climb the Highest Mountain 80

Demonstratives
This, That, These, Those 9
This Is Wednesday, Isn't It? 10
This Can't Be Right 63
Used Car Salesman 69

Future: be + going to
Are You Going To Go With Joe? 50
Hurry Up, Kate! 51
You Ought to Call Your Mother 51

Future: will/won't
Don't Worry, I'll Do It 56
I Hope Jack'll Be There 56
Let's Try 57
I Hope He Won't Be Homesick 57
I've Never Been to Peru, Have You? 74
I'll Climb the Highest Mountain 80

Hope/Wish
I Hope Jack'll Be There 56
I Hope He Won't Be Homesick 57
Can't You Stay for a While? 62

Let's
Let's Try 57
Let's Go Out 58
What Do You Want To Do? 86

Modals: can/could/can't
Don't Worry, I'll Do it 56
Can't Stay, Gotta Go 62
Can't You Stay for a While? 62
This Can't Be Right 63

Modals: have got to/have to
Can't Stay, Gotta Go 62
We've Gotta Get Going 62
This Can't Be Right 63
When Do We Have to Be Back? 64

Modals: ought to/should
You Ought to Call Your Mother 51
What Should I Do? 52
Your Cold Is Getting Worse 68

Object Pronouns

Are You Coming with Us? 15
The Love/Hate Song 20
How Did You Do on the TOEFL Test? 45
What About Me? 50
Are You Going to Go with Joe? 50
You Ought to Call Your Mother 51
Have You Heard the News? 76
I'll Climb the Highest Mountain 80
She Loves Him, but He Doesn't Love Her 86

Past: be

I Was There 32
Where Were You in '62? 32
Wasn't That a Beautiful Wedding? 33
Who Was That Man You Were Talking To? 33
It Was Raining When She Saw Him 34
Wasn't That a Shame? 39

Past: other verbs

Yesterday It Rained and Rained 38
Saturday Morning 44
What's the Matter with Bob? 44
How Did You Do on the TOEFL Test? 45
Logical Questions 45
I Got a Fax From Max 46
Have You Heard the News? 76
Have You Heard from Mary Lately? 76
She loves Him, but He Doesn't Love Her 86
Oh No, We Missed the Bus 87
What's the Matter? 88

Past Continuous

It Was Raining When She Saw Him 34
I Got a Fax from Max 46

Possessives: adjectives/pronouns

Relationships 26
Mistaken Identity 26
Who Was That Man You Were Talking To? 33
Her Laundry Is in the Laundry Bag 38
Where's Jack? 39
Saturday Morning 44
What's the Matter with Bob? 44
Logical Questions 45
Hurry Up, Kate! 51
You Ought to Call Your Mother 51
We've Gotta Get Going 63
Things Are Getting Better 68
Your Cold Is Getting Worse 68

Prepositions

Is There Anybody Here from Thailand? 2
Boxes of Books 4
Where's Mary? 8
Checking In at the Airport 9
When Are You Leaving? 14

Are You Coming with Us? 15
Is She Still Married to Bobby? 16
Relationships 26
He Never Speaks English in His English Class 27
Mistaken Identity 28
Where Were You in '62? 32
Her Laundry Is In the Laundry Bag 38
What's the Matter with Bob? 44
Logical Questions 45
Are You Going to Go with Joe? 50
Have You Ever Been to Boston? 74
He Works Like a Dog 80
Mutual Admiration 81
He's Not the Best 82
When It's Midnight in Osaka 87

Present: be

Are You French? 2
Is There Anybody Here from Thailand? 2
Is Sam Married? 3
Are There Two M's in Grammar? 3
Where's Mary? 8
Checklist 8
Checking In at the Airport 9
This Is Wednesday, Isn't It? 10
Her Laundry Is in the Laundry Bag 38

Present: other verbs

The Love/Hate Song 20
Couch Potato 21
He Loves the Ocean 22
When Do You Usually Have Breakfast? 26
Relationships 26
Habits 27
Let's Go Out 58
He Works Like a Dog 80
Mutual Admiration 82
She Loves Him, but He Doesn't Love Her 86
What's the Matter? 88

Present Continuous

What's Going On This Morning? 14
When Are You Leaving? 14
What's She Doing? 15
Are You Coming With Us? 15
Is She Still Married to Bobby? 16
Where's Jack? 39
Look! The Leaves Are Starting to Fall 40
What About Me? 50
I Hope Jack'll Be There 51
Things Are Getting Better 68
Your Cold Is Getting Worse 68
Life is Getting More and More Complicated 69
The Rich Are Getting Richer 70
Have You Heard From Mary Lately? 76

Present Perfect

Have You Ever Been to Boston? 74
I've Never Been to Peru, Have You? 74
California Roll 75
Have You Heard the News? 76
Have You Heard from Mary Lately? 76
That's the Funniest Thing You've Ever Said 81
What Do You Want to Do? 86

Questions: Yes/No

Are you French? 2
Is There Anybody Here from Thailand? 2
Is Sam Married? 3
Are There Two M's in Grammar? 3
Checklist 8
Checking In at the Airport 9
This Is Wednesday, Isn't It? 10
Are You Coming with Us? 15
Is She Still Married to Bobby? 16
Are You a Student? 20
Couch Potato 21
Do You Always Get Up Early? 21
Mistaken Identity 28
Wasn't That a Beautiful Wedding? 33
Wasn't That a Shame? 39
Are You Going to Go with Joe? 50
This Can't Be Right? 63
Have You Heard the News? 76

Questions: Information

Where's Mary? 8
Checking In at the Airport 9
What's Going on This Morning? 14
When Are You Leaving? 14
What's She Doing? 15
When Do You Usually Have Breakfast? 26
I Was There 32
Where Were You in '62? 32
Who Was That Man You Were Talking To? 33
Where's Jack? 39
What's the Matter with Bob? 44
How Did You Do on the TOEFL Test? 45
Logical Questions 45
I Got a Fax from Max 46
What About Me? 50
You Ought to Call Your Mother 51
What Should I Do? 51
I Hope Jack'll Be There 52
When Do We Have to Be Back? 64
Used Car Salesman 69
Have You Heard the News? 76
What Do You Want to Do? 86
Oh No, We Missed the Bus 87
What's the Matter? 88

Time Expressions

When Are You Leaving? 14
When Do You Usually Have Breakfast? 26
Habits 27
Saturday Morning 44
I Got a Fax from Max 46
Can't You Stay for a While? 62
We've Gotta Get Going 63
Have You Heard from Mary Lately? 76

Structure Index